第八屆亞洲藝術節
The 8th Festival of Asian Arts

香港及澳門風貌
Scenes of Two Cities
Hong Kong & Macau

香港市政局主辦
Presented by the Urban Council, Hong Kong

香港藝術館
Hong Kong Museum of Art
7·10·83 — 20·11·83

ISBN 962-215-052-7
Published by the Urban Council, 1983
Produced by the Hong Kong Museum of Art
7 Edinburgh Place, City Hall, High Block,
Hong Kong

UC 10357
HK$27.00

EXHIBITION MANAGEMENT
Historical Pictures: Joseph S.P. Ting
Publication Design &
Exhibition Graphics: Irene Kho
Exhibition Display: Henri Choi
Photography: Vincent Chan

Contents

Message from the Chairman, Urban Council — 6
Preface — 8
Scenes of Two Cities Hong Kong & Macau — 10
Plates — 17
Contributors — 77

目錄

市政局主席弁言 — 7
序 — 9
香港及澳門風貌 — 14
圖版 — 17
展品借出者 — 77

Message from the Chairman, Urban Council

The Eighth Festival of Asian Arts presents a wide cross-section of traditional and contemporary arts from the Asian and Pacific region. During this 17-day cultural event local audiences and overseas visitors will be able to enjoy a rich spectrum of culture and entertainment.

This year's Festival will, as in past years, reinforce our interest in the cultures around us, and strengthen friendship and mutual understanding among peoples in the region.

Hilton Cheong-Leen
August 9th, 1983

市政局主席弁言

　　第八屆亞洲藝術節節目包括：亞洲與太平洋沿岸地區各種傳統及現代藝術，可謂多采多姿。在十七天藝術節期間，本港和海外觀衆俱獲機緣欣賞豐富而精彩文娛表演。

　　本屆藝術節，一如歷屆，不特加深吾人對亞洲地區各類文化之興趣，抑亦大有助於促進亞洲各地民族友誼和互相了解。

市政局主席張有興
一九八三年八月九日

Preface

It is an apt occasion for the Hong Kong Museum of Art to present an exhibition of historical pictures that visually document the vicissitudes of life during the nineteenth century in the two cosmopolitan cities in Southeast Asia — Hong Kong and Macau in the Eighth Festival of Asian Arts.

This exhibition features a selection of oil paintings, watercolours, prints and drawings on subjects about Hong Kong and Macau selected from the collection in the Hong Kong Museum of Art and several local private collections. Of these, some are the masterpieces of professional artists, while many are the works of the amateurs. Among the more well-known artists included in this exhibition are George Chinnery and Auguste Borget, two of the most significant European artists who visited the two cities and practised their art there. Represented in this exhibition are also the works of the nineteenth century architects G.S. Strachan and Murdoch Bruce and the army draughtsman David Tosswill as well as Commander James Thomas Caldwell, and Captain Robert Elliot. Through their artistic performance we are given the opportunity to learn more about the life activities of the earlier generations in these two cities.

In this exhibition, one cannot escape noticing the dramatic changes of architectural settings as seen in the landscape paintings completed at different times, revealing the rapid metamorphosis of the two places from two semi-barren and primitive fishing villages into two cities of considerable sizes. The different pace of progress and development of the two cities can also be discerned. To-day only a few of the buildings depicted in these pictures still retain their original appearance. In Hong Kong, most of the large impressive early buildings have been demolished. Such landmarks as the Lindsay's and Dent & Co., the Spring Gardens, the Hong Kong Club and the various forts and batteries can now only be contemplated through a tour of these pictorial records. With respect to the preservation of old buildings, Macau enjoys a greater success. Such historical structures as the Misericordia, the facade of the Church of St. Paul and the Ma Kok Temple which were often depicted in landscape paintings of the nineteenth century Macau still stand proudly to be admired by the many visitors of to-day.

We wish to offer a special vote of thanks to the Hong Kong and Shanghai Banking Corporation, Mr R.J.F. Brothers, Mr. & Mrs. Frank Castle and Mr. & Mrs. Peter Thompson for their generous support in contributing their valuable collections for the display. We are most grateful to Mr. Geoffrey Bonsall, our honorary adviser, for his valuable advice. Our thanks are also due to all those who have given assistance in the preparation of this exhibition.

Laurence C.S. Tam
Curator
Hong Kong Museum of Art
August 1983

序

「香港及澳門風貌」是香港藝術館為介紹十九世紀東方兩大都市——香港及澳門的生活面貌而舉辦的歷史畫展覽，這是為配合第八屆亞洲藝術節而舉行的展覽項目之一。

本展覽將展出一系列描繪香港及澳門風貌的油畫、水彩、版畫及素描。這些作品是由到過港澳兩地的職業或業餘畫家所繪畫的。此等畫家中最重要及較著名的有錢納利和波塞爾等。其餘的還有建築師斯特羅恩、布魯士、隨軍繪圖員托斯威爾、海軍將領考德維爾及義律。此等畫家的作品現已成為該時代生活面貌的珍貴圖錄。

不同年代繪畫所見的各類建築，反映了港澳如何從荒僻及落後的漁村蛻變為具規模的都市，展示了兩個城市在不同時代的前進步伐。時光飛逝，當日的建築物許多已無復舊觀。在香港，不少堂皇富麗的建築已告拆卸：林賽洋行、寶順洋行、春園的華廈、香港會所以及一些堡壘砲台祗能從歷史畫得睹昔日原貌。相比之下，澳門的舊建築保存得較多，遠近聞名的仁慈堂、聖保祿教堂的前壁（大三巴），媽閣廟等在歷史畫中常見的古建築至今仍屹立原地，保存完好，為萬千遊人所瞻仰。

本展覽籌辦過程中，得各方鼎力協助，謹此致謝。香港上海滙豐銀行、羅拔•布拉澤斯先生、弗蘭克•卡斯爾先生夫人及彼德•湯普森先生夫人慨允借出珍藏以供展覽，藝術館名譽顧問彭傑福先生提供寶貴意見，謹致衷心謝意。

譚志成
香港藝術館館長
一九八三年八月

Scenes of Two Cities
Hong Kong & Macau

Although the cultural development along the Pearl River started later than that of the other two great cradles of Chinese civilization, the Yellow River and the Yangtze River, it was in the delta area in the lower tributaries of the Pearl River that China first came into contact with modern western civilization and it was there that an important chapter in the history of East-West cultural and economic exchange took place. Situated not far from the mouth of the Pearl River, Hong Kong and Macau oversee the strategic maritime access leading to Guangzhou, the economic and cultural centre of South China, like two door gods guarding the southern gate of China.

Early in the middle of the sixteenth century, the Portuguese traders traversed the Cape of Good Hope to reach the Orient. They finally picked the fishing port Macau where they later obtained a land lease to settle and develop it as a trading post.[1] Three centuries later the British, who had established a predominate control of the sea-trade, acquired Hong Kong, the small island east of Macau, as a spring-board to the China Trade. Today Hong Kong has developed into a cosmopolitan city while Macau also prospered in a glorious past two centuries earlier. The two cities have played different roles in different periods of time but the prolonged presence of foreigners has tinted both cities with peculiarly foreign overtones.

The urban development of Macau much predates that of Hong Kong. During the fourteenth and fifteenth centuries, the trade route from Asia Minor to the East was blocked by the Turks. The Spanish and the Portuguese painstakingly sought a new trading route to the Orient. After the discovery of the Cape of Good Hope by Bartholomeo Dias and Vasco da Gama, Portuguese influence extended into the Orient and gradually succeeded in gaining control over trade in the South China Sea. The Portuguese were at first very active in the area around Lampakkau (an island near Macau) and Sanchuan (St John's Island). Later, as a reward for their assistance in combating pirates, it is said that the Ming Government granted them the right to establish residence in Macau.[2] The subsequent emergence of an urban settlement was the result of the building of a trading port, massive construction and an influx of merchants and traders from neightbouring regions. Thus was founded the earliest foothold for westerners in China.

During the period from the sixteenth to the mid-seventeenth century, the Ming Court prohibited her coastal subjects from trading with the Japanese. With Macau as their base, the Portuguese gradually dominated the trade between Goa and Japan. Macau was at its zenith.[3] This was the time when the magnificent St Paul's Church was constructed.

However, the golden epoch of Macau did not last long. Following the footsteps of the Portuguese, the Spanish and the Dutch also came east and gained control of the Philippines, Java and Taiwan. Great economic setback soon ensued when the Portuguese were expelled from Japan for suspected complicity in a riot in Nagasaki. Moreover, Portugal and Spain were at odds and Macau lost its lucrative position as the entrepot in the trade between China, Japan and the Philippines. While Portugal was plagued by internal dissension, the city of Macau was attacked and besieged by the Dutch. Although the Macanese succeeded in defending the city against the Dutch assaults, Macau was never able to recover its previous prosperity.[4]

In 1757, Emperor Qianlong ordered all ports closed except Guangzhou. Merchants from England, France, Holland, Sweden, Denmark and Spain were allowed to stay in the Factories in Guangzhou during the winter season, but they had to leave for Macau in the off-trade season in summer. Morever, as women and children were forbidden in the Factories, they were compelled to reside in Macau which became a European foothold outside Guangzhou. This in fact brought new hope to Macau which was struggling on the brink of economic bankruptcy. In 1849 the Governor, Amaral, declared Macau a free port in the hope of bringing a reversal of the declining economy of Macau. Unfortunately, Amaral's attempt only led to his tragic assassination.[5] The whole community was in disarray and many Portuguese left for Hong Kong.[6]

Macau has been occupied by the Portuguese for over four hundred years. This long period of Portuguese rule has imbued the city with a pronounced western favour. The Catholic cathedral and the many churches, the cobbled streets, the sturdy fortifications are seldom found in other places in the Orient. Most of the architecture in Macau is an ingenious stylistic mixture of East and West. The facade of the Church of St Paul is inscribed in both Latin and Chinese and is carved with chrysanthemums representing Japan and dragon representing China. Roofed with Chinese tile, the Church of St Lawrence is decorated with terracotta panels. Similarly, the Church and Seminary of St Joseph is also topped with tiled roof. The local buildings also exhibit the amalgamation of Chinese and western influences: tiled, pitched roofs are hidden behind parapets and balustrades in a Renaissance style, external walls emulate western designs in stucco, the addition of verandahs and balconies, windows with adjustable-shutter screens that are very suitable for the sub-tropical climate, semi-circular lintels in the verandahs, interior decoration following traditional Chinese lines, and doorways, portals, skirtings, cornices, friezes, etc., that tend increasingly to depict western motifs.[7]

Before the coming of the Portuguese, Macau was a fishing village. Most of the fisherfolks would erect thatched huts along the coast or shelters on stilts along the shores against the rain and the wind. Splendid villas were later introduced by the Portuguese on the Praya Grande while the Chinese population congregated in the area around the Inner Harbour and the coastal area west of Camoes Gardens. Therefore, the small peninsula had both the alluring sentiments of idyllic European romanticism as well as the enchanting lyricism of an eastern fishing village and attracted numerous travellers from the seventeenth century onwards. The Chinese was especially drawn by the foreign sights and sounds of Macau. The Late Ming poet Qu Dajun was fascinated by the attire and customs of the Portuguese: "They take off their felt hats for greetings, their body wrapt in rich brocade, sabre by their side, hair down their shoulders."[8] The painter Wu Li found the thrill and excitement of the Christmas celebration in Macau especially fascinating: "In chandeliers and chandeliers the small isle glistens, with silk and satin as cloudranges heaving the candles blossom. Rouge colours the wintry hills in joyous jubilation, Negroes dance the rhythm of pipa chiming celebration."[9] Moreover, the notable Late Qing politician Wei Yuan pointed out that "the gardens and pavilions of Macau awe one with the feeling of travelling overseas". He had been a house guest in a Portuguese household and was much enticed by a western woman's piano recital.[10]

The westerners were equally interested in Chinese customs. The main points of attraction for them were the fisherfolks of Macau, the thatched cottages, the crowded market places, the exuberant Ma Kok Temple, pedlars, beggars, and pigs, etc. The French painter Auguste Borget reached South China in 1838 during his journey around the world and resided in Macau for half a year. All the particulars he observed in Macau were entered into his travelogue in vivid detail and many of his oil paintings and sketches recorded the scenery of Macau.[11] George Chinnery, an English artist, was particularly infatuated with Macau. After moving to Macau, it was said that he did sketches outdoors everyday. From his numerous watercolours and sketches extant today, we can discern the artist's intense interest in the Chinese way of living: the mobile barber shop, food stands, gambling stalls, and blacksmiths, were all subjects of his paintings and sketches. Among them, the fisherfolks living along the coast was a favourite subject for Chinnery. In his description of the China expedition of Lord Elgin, the Englishman Laurence Oliphant has the following impression of Macau, "The narrow streets and grass-grown plazas, the handsome facade of the fine old cathedral crumbling to decay, the shady walks and cool grottoes, once the haunt of the Portuguese Poet; his tomb, and the view from it, all combine to produce a soothing and tranquillising effect upon sensibilities irritated by our recent mode of life."[12] The alluring scenery of Macau is vividly depicted.

The urban development of Hong Kong took place much later than that of Macau. During the eighteenth and the early nineteenth century, the British merchants spent their long, hot summers in Macau. Residences were rented by the English East India Company to accommodate its staff.[13] Later, as the hostility between China and Britain intensified, it became increasingly difficult for the British to reside in Macau. British merchants were thus compelled to go to Hong Kong where they briefly lived on board the ships anchored off Tsim Sha Tsui. The most pressing need then was to find an island near the estuary of the Pearl River as their trading base. In the early nineteenth century, most of the British trading vessels to China obtained drinking water from the waterfall at Shek Pai Wan. They had already discovered that the island was an ideal trading base as the supply of fresh water was plentiful and to the north was a fine deep harbour. Following the Convention of Chuenpi agreed between Keshen and Captain Charles Elliot, the British Naval Commander Sir Gordon Bremer took possession of Hong Kong on January 26, 1841. Hong Kong thus entered a new epoch and drastic changes ensued.

Although Hong Kong became a British Crown Colony only after the Chinese Commissioner Keying arrived in Hong Kong to exchange the documents of the Treaty of Nanking with the governor, Sir Henry Pottinger in June 1843, construction work has already commenced well before then. In November 1841, the hillside between the Albany and Glenealy nullah was officially named Government Hill, as the site for the construction of government buildings.[14] The subsequent construction of the Government Offices (1849), Government House (1855), St John's Cathedral (1849), and the Albany Quarters were all congregated in this area. The large patch of land extending from the hillside on the east to Wanchai was earmarked by the Armed Forces for the building of barracks. The famous Flagstaff House, the official residence of the Commander of the British Forces was erected on the hilltop east of the Albany nullah. This town planning scheme which was laid down right after the British takeover confined commercial and residential development to the west of the Government Hill and the Barracks to the east. This obstruction of the Government Hill and the Barracks in the middle of the island blocked off the eastern and western areas in their urban development, each taking its independent course. The situation remained unchanged for over a hundred years until the very recent past.

Lying adjacent to Government Hill, the Central district is the heart of the city. Lindsay's Company and Dent & Co. purchased the marine lots in the first land auction in June 1841 and began their extensive construction projects of godowns and offices. The Harbour Master's office was built on the small hill west of Battery Path overlooking the harbour. The hill was named Pedder's Hill after the first Harbour Master, Lieut William Pedder. The social centre of upper class westerners, the Hong Kong Club, was situated at the foot of Pedder's Hill on the present Queen's Road. While most of the westerners resided along the foothills around Pottinger Street, Wellington Street and Lyndhurst Terrace, the Chinese congregated in the Western Districts and Tai Ping Shan area. The segregation continued until the late nineteenth century when Chinese residents crossed over Aberdeen Street and extended eastwards into the European residential area.

In the nineteenth century, most of the population of Hong Kong island was concentrated in the areas around the Central and Western Districts, Saiyingpoon and Tai Ping Shan. It was much scattered east of the Barracks. During the early stage of urban development, Spring Gardens was a nicely situated upper class residential area in Wanchai. To the east are Hospital Hill and Morrison Hill.[15] The valley behind Morrison Hill was originally swamp and fields. The government initially contemplated much construction on the site, but the proposition was abandoned due to poor hygenic conditions, and the valley was later used for cemeteries and a horse-racing track. To the east of Morrison Hill is East Point, which had been bought by Jardine, Matheson & Co. The Company commenced the construction of godowns, piers and office buildings there in 1842. In 1844 the headquarters of the Company was moved from Macau to Hong Kong. Until the late nineteenth century, the area east of East Point remained undeveloped. There were only few fishermen's dwellings in Quarry Bay. Stanley and Shek Pai Wan on the south coast were also modest fishing villages.

The population of Hong Kong increased steadily from the mid-nineteenth century. Houses were built along the hillside forming a scene of one row of buildings erected upon each contour. The phenomenon surprised travellers from Mainland China. The scholar Wei Yuan compared it to "the celestrial palace in the Penglai fairyland."[16] The calligrapher and poet, He Shaoji commented, "The multi-layered houses and pavilions were extravagantly displayed. The dress and adornment are all non-Chinese in fashion."[17] On the other hand, the poet Wang Zunxian wrote ten expressive poems on Hong Kong on his first visit to the island in 1870. "Embroiled in a sea of music and songs, mountains overflowing with meat and wine. Tens of thousand of dwellings laced the rolling hills. Each square feet is worth over one thousand gold. The local custom is much affected with foreign influence."[18] These comments already gave the impression of the increasing affluence of the wealthy Chinese merchants, the growing scarcity of land and the expanding populace. After an extended stay in Hong Kong, the reformist politician Wang Tao made some acute observations. In "A Brief Account of Hong Kong", he said, "The numerous buildings in Hong Kong are compactly placed. Their disposition follows the contour of the hills. Its irregularity resembles a row of flying geese." He also had the following comments on the living conditions of the Chinese around the Tai Ping Shan Area: "The dwellings of the Chinese locals are often small snail shells. The crowded condition is comparable to that of a bee-hive. Each floor houses as many as seven to eight households or at least two to three. Sharing under the same roof but cooking in individual stoves, they live like silkworms in the cocoon and caterpillars in the den."[19] After seeing "the splendor of the buildings, the orderly array of the roads, and the solemn appearance of the police force," the champion of the Hundred Day Reform movement during the Late Qing period, Kang Yuwei greatly admired the ruling strategy of the European.[20]

The galloping development of Hong Kong came as a surprise even to the western visitors and traders. The Rev. George Smith considered Hong Kong a close resemblance to towns on the European continent.[21] Captain Arthur Cunynghame said, "In August 1841, not one single house was yet built, not a portion of the brush-wood had been cleared away from this desolate spot. By June 1842, the town was considerably more than two miles long, containing store-houses and shops, here called 'Godowns' in which almost every article either Eastern or European could be procured, and most of them, at not very unreasonable prices."[22] However, most of the westerners found life in Hong Kong too dull and bland. Laurence said, "When it was not blowing or raining, the heat was intolerable; and we all suffered more or less in health from its evil effects. Often for days together we remained sweltering on board, from lack of energy or sufficient inducement to leave the ship.... The monotony of life is varied by this malady alternating with boils or dysentry.... It was not difficult to account for a certain depression of spirits, and tone of general irritability, which seemed to pervade the community."[23] When the painter Auguste Borget passed through Hong Kong in 1838, it was still a modest fishing village. But in 1846, when George Chinnery visited Hong Kong, it had already become a city of imposing scale. The waterfront area along the Central District was practically "buildings and pavilions rising with the clouds in mid air". Chinnery only spent one summer in Hong Kong. The city's fascination for him was not as great as Macau. It can be seen in the few existing sketches, oil and watercolour paintings which Chinnery executed during his brief stay in Hong Kong that the island was in a phase of active construction. Common scenes in his paintings are stonecutters levelling mountains and clearing land for construction work. The two followers of George Chinnery, Dr Thomas B. Watson and Marciano A. Baptista, also executed many paintings showing views of Hong Kong. While Dr Watson painted as a pastime, the Macau born Baptista sold paintings for a living and thus left a larger number of them. His paintings are notable for their accuracy of depiction. He had a predilection for painting the Central and harbour scenes as a bird's-eye view from the Mid-levels showing the jungle of sailboat masts and one row of buildings erected upon each contour. Other painters who passed through Hong Kong during the nineteenth century included John H. Collins, R. Shannon, Robert G.D. Tosswill, Edward Hilderbrandt, Lieut Walford T. Bellairs, among others. They were all amateur painters. As most of them were naval draughsmen, their technique in painting cannot be compared with that of Borget and Chinnery. However, they have given us scenes of Hong Kong from different perspectives and at varying times. The works they left are thus historical testimony to the spectacular growth of Hong Kong in the nineteenth century.

During the nineteenth century, Laurence Oliphant, the author of *Narrative of the Earl of Elgin's Mission to China and Japan in the years 1857*, made several brief sojourns in both Hong Kong and Macau each only lasting a few days. The impression he got was: "Its (Macau's) air of respectable antiquity was refreshing, after the somewhat parvenu character with which its ostentatious magnificence invests Hong Kong."[24] The opinion of Oliphant in fact represented the feeling of most of the westerners who visited the two cities and perhaps explains why Chinnery preferred to stay in Macau. Although the two cities are not far apart and both are under European sovereignty, the totally different moods and sentiments of Hong Kong and Macau left quite different impressions on the mind of the nineteenth century visitors and to some extent still do so today.

Joseph S.P. Ting
Assistant Curator
August, 1983

Notes

1. 'Folangji juan' (History of the Portuguese Activities in China) in *Mingshi* (Ming History), Shanghai, p.12b.
2. According to Chinese literary records, the Portuguese had bribed Wang Qing, the commander of Guangzhou with a considerable amount of money in order to get the permission to rent Macau as a foothold for their trading activities. *Ibid.*
3. Cf. Austin Coates, *A Macau Narrative*, Hong Kong, Heinemann, 1978, Ch. 3.
4. Cf. *Ibid.*, Ch. 5.
5. Cf. *Ibid.*, Ch. 7.
6. G.B. Endacott, *A History of Hong Kong*, London, Oxford University Press, 1958, p.85.
7. Cf. *Hong Kong Going and Gone*, Hong Kong, The Hong Kong Branch of the Royal Asiastic Society, 1980, p.1.
8. Cf. Qu Dajun, *Guangdong xinyu* (A Miscellany of Guangdong), Vol. 2, Hong Kong, 1974, p.37.
9. Wu Li, 'Aozhong Zayong' (Ode to Macau), in *Sanba ji* (A Macau Collection), 1874 edition, Vol. 13, p.4b.
10. Wei Yuan, 'Aomen huayuan ting yinu yanqin ge' (Listening to the piano recital given by a western woman in a Macau garden), in Huang Yu, *Lidai mingren ru Yue shixuan* (A Collection of Poems by Eminent Persons who have visited Guangzhou), Guangzhou, Guangdong People's Publishers, 1980, p.446.
11. Auguste Borget, *Sketches of China and the Chinese*, London, Tilt and Bogue, 1842.
12. Quoted from Laurence Oliphant, *Narrative of the Earl of Elgin's Mission to China and Japan in the years 1857*, London, William Blackwood and Sons, 1860, p.67.
13. During the late eighteenth century, the British rented the house of Mr Manuel Pereira in the Camoes Gardens as the residence for the Superintendent of the English East Indian Company. The English Ambassadors Lord Amherst and Lord Macartney lived there during their visit to China. The house was converted into a museum in 1960. The building opposite the Church of St. Lawrence was also at one time rented as the residence of the Chief of the English East Indian Company at Guangzhou. See J.M. Braga, 'Hong Kong and Anglo-Portuguese Amity', *Noticias De Macau*, 1951.
14. Cf. Dafydd M.E. Evans, 'The Foundation of Hong Kong: A Chapter of Accidents', in *Hong Kong: The Interaction of Traditions and Life in the Towns*, edited by Marjorie Topley, Hong Kong, Hong Kong Branch of the Royal Asiastic Society, 1972.
15. Early in 1842, Sir Henry Pottinger allotted the two hills neighbouring Wanchai to the Morrison Educational Society and the Medical Missionary Society to build a school and a hospital. From then on the two hills were named Morrison Hill and Hospital Hill respectively.
16. See footnote 10, 'Xianggangdao guan hai shi ge' (Song on the Sea and City Scenes of Hong Kong), p.447.
17. He Shaoji, 'Cheng huochuan you Aomen yu Xianggang zuo, wangfan sanri, yue shuicheng sanshi li' (Composed when travelling between Macau and Hong Kong by ferry, back and forth for about three days, and covering a distance of about two kilometres), in Huang Yu, *Lidai mingren ru Yue shixuan* (A Collection of Poems by Eminent Persons who have visited Guangzhou), p.450.
18. Xianggang Ganhuaishi Shishou (Ten Lyrics Poems on Hong Kong), *Renjinglu shicao jianzhu* (Notes and commentary on Poems of Renjinglu), Shanghai, 1981, p.69.
19. Wang Tao, 'Xianggang Luelun' (A Brief Account of Hong Kong), in *Manyou suilu* (Jottings of a Wandering Trip); quoted from Lin Yu-lan, *Xianggang shi hua* (A Brief History of Hong Kong), Hong Kong, 1980, p.81, footnote 2.
20. Quoted from Luo Xianglin, *Xianggang yu zhongxi wenhua zhi jiaoliu* (Hong Kong and the East-West Cultural Interflow), Hong Kong, 1961, p.73, footnote 45.
21. Quoted from James Orange, *The Chater Collection*, London, 1924, p.337.
22. Orange, *op. cit.*, p.334.
23. Orange, *op. cit.*, p.65.
24. *Ibid.*

香港及澳門風貌

黃河、長江及珠江是中國三大主要河流。黃河及長江流域是中國文化的搖籃。珠江流域開發較晚，但其下游三角洲一帶，却是最早接觸近代西方文明的地方，在近代中外通商及文化交流史上佔着重要的一頁。位於珠江口兩岸的澳門及香港，監視扼守着通向華南經濟文化中心——廣州必經的水道，是守衛中國南大門的一對門神。

早在十六世紀中葉，遠渡重洋到東方貿易的葡萄牙人便選中澳門這個漁港，租地定居[1]，發展貿易。三個世紀後，執海上貿易牛耳的英國人也取得澳門彼岸的香港，作為對華貿易的跳板。香港現已發展為國際性的大都市，而澳門在二個多世紀前也有過一段輝煌的歲月。兩個地方在不同的歷史時期擔演過不同的角色。西方人長時期的統治，使這兩個城市洋溢着獨特的異國色彩。

澳門開埠歷史遠比香港為早。十四、十五世紀時，小亞細亞到東方貿易的商路為土耳其人所遮斷，葡萄牙及西班牙的君主貴族乃積極向東方尋求新的貿易通路。在地亞士及瓦斯高‧達伽馬等人開闢好望角航路後，葡人的勢力進入東方世界，逐漸控制了南海貿易的主權。葡人曾在浪白澫及上川一帶活動，後因協助明朝政府緝捕海盜有功，獲准於澳門居留[2]，設港通商，築城造房。鄰近的商人小販亦聞風而至，遂聚眾成市，成為西方人在中國最早的立足點。

十六世紀至十七世紀中葉這段時期，適值明廷禁止沿海人民與日本通商，葡人乃以澳門為中心，控制印度臥亞及東瀛間的貿易。這是澳門歷史上的黃金時代[3]。巍峨壯麗的聖保祿教堂(大三巴)就是在這個時期建造的。

但好景不常，繼葡人之後，西班牙及荷蘭人也先後東來，並分別佔據了菲律賓群島、爪哇及台灣。另一方面，日本德川幕府懷疑葡人煽動長崎日人作亂，驅逐葡人，加上葡國與西班牙交惡，澳門遂失去了作為中國、日本及菲島之間貨物轉運站的地位，經濟情況乃一落千丈。在此時期，澳門曾受到荷蘭人的襲擊，加上葡國本土內亂，使澳門元氣大傷[4]。

一七五七年乾隆下令封鎖其他海港，專限廣州一處與外國貿易。從英國、法國、荷蘭、瑞典、丹麥及西班牙來的商人，冬天住在廣州的商館，而夏天却需住到澳門去。當時的廣州商館是不准女眷居住的，外商的家屬均需留在澳門，澳門乃成為西方商人在廣州以外的立足點。這個情況，給沉滯一時的澳門帶來新的希望。一八四九年澳督亞馬勒斷然宣佈澳門為自由港，力圖挽回澳門的經濟頹勢。結果，亞馬勒的行動為自己招惹殺身之禍[5]，澳門亦因而陷入恐慌中，不少葡人更於此時移居香港[6]。

澳門開埠至今已超過四百年，長期的葡國統治，給這個地方披上濃厚的西洋色彩。鱗次櫛比的天主堂，滿鋪小石的馬路，堅固的炮台，都是在東方其他地方看不到的。澳門的古建築，不少是東西風格混合的產物。如聖保祿教堂前壁不單刻有拉丁文，更刻有中文，壁上還雕有代表日本的菊花及中國的龍。風順堂(聖老楞佐堂)頂鋪瓦面，還飾以中國陶版。而聖約瑟修院(三巴仔)也鋪上瓦面。至於一般建築，更結合了中西建築形式：屋頂鋪瓦，四面是文藝復興期流行的女牆和欄杆，外髹為白灰牆，設游廊及露台，窗戶多採用百葉窗，以適應澳門潮濕而炎熱的氣候。走廊門楣作圓拱形，內部裝飾是中國式，而門柱、門楣及前壁的紋飾多為西洋風格[7]。

葡人未來之前，澳門原為一漁村，漁民們在岸上蓋搭茅寮或在海邊築起棚屋以蔽風雨。葡人來到後，選擇南灣沿岸一帶興建高棟飛甍的洋房，而華人則多聚居於內港及白鴿巢以西海邊地區，所以這個面積不大的半島，既有歐洲浪漫閒恬的迷人情調，也有東方漁村的旖旎風光，自十七世紀以來，吸引過無數的遊人。中國人最嚮往的是濠江的異國風情。比方晚明的詩人屈大均對葡人「以黑氈為帽，相見脫之以為禮，錦綢裹身，腰帶長刀，其髮垂至肩」的裝束及禮俗留下深刻印象[8]。而畫家吳歷則注意到澳門人慶祝聖誕「百千燈耀小林崖，錦作雲巒蠟作花，粧點冬山齊慶賀，黑人舞足應琵琶」的熱鬧景況[9]。晚清著名的經學家魏源更指出濠江的「園亭樓閣，如游海外」，他在澳門曾作客於葡人家中，聆聽夷女彈奏洋琴，非常陶醉[10]。

西方人的興趣，當然與中國人不同，他們留意的是濠江的漁民、茅寮、肩摩轂擊的市集、瑰麗璀璨的媽閣廟，以及隨處可見的各類小販、乞丐、豬隻……。法國畫家波塞爾在東遊途中，於一八三八年抵達華南，在澳門住了半年之久。其遊記對澳門的一景一物都有極生動的描寫。而他的油畫及素描，更繪畫出目視的景象[11]。英國畫家錢納利對澳門更是情有獨鐘，他在一八二五年自印度移居澳門後，便一直以澳門為家。香港開埠後，原居住於澳門的英人紛紛遷港，但錢氏仍寧選澳門為終老之地。據說他每天都出外寫生，從他現存大量的水彩及素描可體會到他對華人生活的無比興趣：流動的街頭理髮檔、食物檔、賭檔、鐵匠都是他描繪的對象；而居住於海濱的蜑民，更是錢納利特別喜愛的題材。英人奧利芬特在其叙述額爾金勛爵訪華的紀錄中對澳門的風光有如下描述：「狹窄的街道、野草叢生的廣場、古老教堂的壯觀前壁、葡國詩人（賈梅士）以前常漫步的林蔭小徑及清凉的洞穴，都無比迷人。而從賈氏的墳塋游目四望，如詩如畫的景色可鬆馳現代緊張的生活[12]。」澳門的醉人風光，躍然紙上。

香港開埠比澳門晚得多。在十八及十九世紀初期，英國商人都是在澳門渡過炎炎長夏的。英國東印度公司也在澳門租賃若干樓宇供公司職員住宿[13]。在中英啓釁後，英國人再不能居留澳門，乃浮海而東，棲身於停泊在尖沙咀對開的船舶上。故設法取得珠江口附近一個島嶼作立足之所，乃成為當務之急。早在十九世紀初，英國商人來華貿易的船隻，多在石排灣附近一條山坑取水食用。他們發現這個海島水源充足，北面是一個深水的良港，是一個理想的據點。一八四一年一月廿六日，英艦隊司令伯麥根據義律及琦善簽訂的穿鼻草約接管香港。這個荒蕪的漁村未幾便發生翻天覆地的變化。

雖然在一八四三年六月欽差大使耆英涖港和砵典乍交換南京條約文件，香港才正式成為英國殖民地；但在此之前，香港島的建設已告展開。一八四一年十一月，港府把雅賓利和忌連拿利渠道之間的山坡定名為「政府山」，留作興建政府建築之用[14]。後來的輔政司署（一八四九）、督憲府（一八五五）、聖約翰教堂（一八四九），以至雅賓利政府公務員宿舍（一八四四）都集中在這個地區。而東面山坡伸延至灣仔的一大片土地，却被軍部圈為興築軍營之用。著名的建築旗杆屋——舊三軍司令官邸就矗立於雅賓利溝渠以東一個山頭上。這個開埠伊始便釐定的城市規劃決定了商業及住宅區祇能循政府山以西或軍部以東的地區拓展。百多年來，政府山及英軍軍區橫亘港島中央，分隔了城市發展的局面一直維持下來，至最近才有改變。

與政府山毗鄰的中環，是城市的心臟地帶。在一八四一年六月首次土地競投中，寶順及林賽等洋行便購入了海濱地段，興建貨倉及寫字樓。港務局就設在砲台徑西鄰一個可俯瞰港海的山崗之上，這個山就以第一位港務局長畢打命名。西人上層社會的社交中心——香港會所就設於畢打山脚。大部份的洋人住在靠山的砵典乍街、威靈頓街及擺花街一帶。至於華人則聚居於上環、太平山街地區。彼此涇渭分明，至十九世紀晚期，華人才越過鴨巴甸街，向東伸展入歐人住宅區。

在十九世紀，港島的人口以中環、上環、西營盤及太平山一帶最為集中。軍部以東人口較為分散。開埠之初，春園是環境優美的濱海高尚住宅區，其東面是醫院山及摩利臣山[15]。摩利臣山背後的山谷，原為一片田疇及沼澤地帶。開埠初期，當局曾一度考慮在該處大興土木，但終因衞生條件不佳而放棄，改作為墳地及跑馬場。摩利臣山以東的東角是渣甸洋行的天地。一八四二年該洋行在這裏動工興建倉庫、碼頭及辦公大樓。一八四四年，渣甸的總部從澳門遷至香港。直至十九世紀末，東角以東的地區還是很荒蕪，祇有筲箕灣有些漁民聚居。南岸的赤柱及石排灣亦是樸素的漁村。

十九世紀中葉以後，香港的人口逐年遞增。屋宇沿着山邊興建，形成「一層坡嶺一層屋」的情況。內地過港人士，無不驚異，經學家魏源比之為「蓬萊宮闕」[16]。書法家、詩人何紹基更有「層樓叠閣金碧麗，服飾全非中土制」的評語[17]。詩人黃遵憲在一八七〇年初到香港，寫了十首香港感懷詩，有「沸地笙歌海，排山酒肉林，連環屯萬室，尺土過千金，民氣多羶行」等句[18]，可知當時香港的華人富商，生活漸趨豪奢，而地狹人多，寸金尺土的現象已經出現。改良主義政治家王韜在香港住過較長時期，他的觀察更為深入，在《香港略論》指出：「港中之屋，鱗次櫛比，隨山高下，參差如雁戶」。他對太平山一帶香港華人的環境有如下描述：「華民所居率多小如蝸舍，密若蜂房……一屋中多者常至七八家，少亦二三家，同居異爨……有若蠶之在繭，蠖之蟄穴，非復人類所居。」[19] 至於晚清鼓吹維新的康有為則因目睹「宮室之壯麗，道路之整潔、巡捕之嚴肅」而對歐人之治術佩服不已[20]。

香港發展之迅速，連西方來的商人遊客都感到驚異。香港會督喬治・史密斯牧師認為香港看似一個歐陸的市鎮[21]。阿瑟・坎尼咸說：「在一八四一年八月，連一間房屋都沒有，到處是密林野草，一八四二年六月，這個城市已超過兩哩長，滿佈貨庫及商店，各類中西貨品齊備，價錢也不太昂貴。」[22] 但他們多認為香港的生活枯燥無味，奧利芬特說：「沒有風也沒有雨的日子，熱浪迫人，每個人都感到不適。我們常多日留在船上，提不起勁上岸……生活單調，人們常染上疾病——長癬子或痢疾。整個社會瀰漫着一片低落的氣氛。」[23] 波塞爾在一八三八年過港時，香港還是一個樸素的漁村。到錢納利一八四六年訪港時，香港已頗具規模，中區海旁一帶已儼然是個「半空樓閣連雲起」的新興城市了。錢氏祇在香港住了一個夏天，顯然這個城市對他的吸引力遠不如澳門，從錢氏現存數目不多的居港時所作的油畫、水彩及素描可知當時香港正處於積極建設階段。畫面到處可看到石匠在開山鑿地，從事建設。錢納利的兩個弟子屈臣醫生及巴普蒂斯塔也繪畫了不少香港風景畫。其中屈臣醫生祇是以之消閒，而在澳門出生的巴氏却以鬻畫維生的。巴氏存世畫作較多，其作品以描繪精確見稱。他喜歡以俯瞰方式在半山繪畫中區及海港景色，突出港海帆檣如林及沿山「一層坡嶺一層屋」的景象。十九世紀到過香港的畫家包括柯林斯、香農、托斯威爾、希爾德布蘭德、貝萊爾斯等，都是業餘畫家，其中大部份是海軍繪圖員。他們的技巧，自然不能與波、錢等人相提並論，但他們在不同時期來港，從不同角度繪畫各處不同的景貌，此等作品乃是十九世紀香港飛躍發展的歷史見證。

奧利芬特在十九世紀中葉曾先後在香港及澳門盤桓過數天。他的印象是：「遊過十里洋場近似暴發戶一般的香港，更深深體會到澳門所瀰漫着的古雅氣氛，份外使人心曠神怡[24]。」奧氏的看法相信代表了不少十九世紀到過香港和澳門兩地的西方人士的心聲，也解釋了錢氏寧長居澳門的原因。香港及澳門雖然相距不遠，且同為歐人統治下的地方，但兩地的風光及情調，在十九世紀遊人心目中留下的印象却大相迴異。

丁新豹
助理館長
一九八三年八月

注釋

注一　見《明史》，《佛朗機傳》，上海中華書局四部備要版，一九三四年，頁十二下。

注二　根據中國文獻記載，一五三五年（明嘉靖十四年）葡商以巨賄勾結廣州指揮黃慶，租借澳門為通商根據地，事見《明史》，卷三二五，《佛朗機傳》，上海中華書局四部備要版，一九三四年，頁十二下。

注三　參考 Austin Coates, *A Macau Narrative*, Heinemann, 香港，一九七八年版，第三章。

注四　同上書，第五章。

注五　同上書，第七章。

注六　見 G.B. Endacott, *A History of Hong Kong*, Oxford University Press, 倫敦，一九五八年版，頁八五。

注七　參考 *Hong Kong Going and Gone*, The Hong Kong Branch of the Royal Asiastic Society, 香港，一九八〇年版，頁一。

注八　參見屈大均：《廣東新語》，卷二，中華書局，香港一九七四年版，頁三七。

注九　見吳歷：《三巴集》，《澳中雜咏》，小石山房叢書，同治十三年版，第十三冊，頁四下。

注十　見魏源所作之《澳門花園聽夷女洋琴歌》，收入黃雨：《歷代名人入粵詩選》，廣東人民出版社，一九八〇年版，頁四四六。

注十一　Auguste Borget, *Sketches of China and the Chinese*, Tilt and Bogue, 倫敦，一八四二年版。

注十二　引自 Laurence Oliphant, *Narrative of the Earl of Elgin's Mission to China and Japan in the years 1857*, William Blackwood and Sons, 倫敦，一八六〇年版，頁六七。

注十三　十八世紀末葉，英國人租賃了葡人佩雷拉在白鴿巢的洋房，作為英國東印度公司主席委員之住宅。英使阿默斯特及馬戛爾尼訪華途經澳門時曾住在這裏。房子在一九六〇年改為博物館，而風順堂對面的「十六柱」，也曾是東印度公司負責人的私邸。見 J.M. Braga, 'Hong Kong and Anglo-Portuguese Amity', *Noticias De Macau*, 澳門，一九五一年版。

注十四　參考 Dafydd M.E. Evans, The Foundation of Hong Kong: A Chapter of Accidents 收入 Marjorie Topley 編之 *Hong Kong: The Interaction of Traditions and Life in the Towns*, Hong Kong Branch of the Royal Asiastic Society, 香港，一九七二年版。

注十五　一八四二年初砵典乍把下環（灣仔）附近的兩個山岡，分別撥給馬禮遜教育會及傳道醫療會興築醫院及學校。從此，這兩個山就分別被稱為摩利臣山及醫院山。

注十六　見注十，頁四四七之《香港島觀海市歌》。

注十七　見何紹基所作之《乘火輪船游澳門與香港作，往返三日，約水程二千里》，收入黃雨：《歷代名人入粵詩選》，廣東人民出版社，一九八〇年版，頁四五〇。

注十八　見《香港感懷詩十首》，黃遵憲：《人境廬詩草箋注》，上海古籍出版社，一九八一年版，頁六九。

注十九　見王韜：《香港略論》，收入《漫遊隨錄》，轉引自林友蘭：《香港史話》，香港，一九八〇年版。頁八一，注二。

注二十　轉引自羅香林：《香港與中西文化之交流》，中國學社，香港，一九六一年版，頁七三，註四五。

注廿一　轉引自 James Orange, *The Chater Collection*, 倫敦，一九二四年版，頁三三七。

注廿二　同上，頁三三四。

注廿三　同注十二，頁六五。

注廿四　同上。

1
A Village Shrine by the Roadside, Hong Kong, 1838
by Auguste Borget, 1809-1877
pencil drawing on paper, 19.5 × 30.5cm
signed and inscribed in French, Little Altar by the Side of the Road in the Bay of Hong Kong, 24 August 1838

This painting inscribed in French, 24 August 1838, was done the day after the French artist Auguste Borget arrived at Hong Kong on board the frigate ''Psyche'' on August 23, 1838.

香港的路邊「社公」，一八三八年
波塞爾畫（一八〇九至一八七七）
紙本鉛筆素描　19.5×30.5厘米
附有畫家署名及題識

法國畫家波塞爾在一八三八年八月廿三日乘「西奇」號輪抵香港，是圖題有「一八三八年八月廿四日」字樣，可知爲抵港翌日所繪。「社公」是中國民間所信仰的神祇之一。

2
A Chinese Funeral Ceremony, Hong Kong, 1838
by Auguste Borget, 1809-1877
oil painting, 33 × 52cm

Borget witnessed a Chinese funeral ceremony the third day after his arrival in Hong Kong. He published a detailed account of what he saw in *Sketches of China and the Chinese*.

葬禮，一八三八年
波塞爾畫(一八〇九至 一八七七)
油畫　33×52厘米

波塞爾在抵香港後的第三天，看到一個華人葬禮，他把所見紀錄在「中國及中國人素描集」一書中。

3
Early View of the Government Hill, 1841
by John H. Collins
watercolour on paper, 23.6 × 32cm
signed and inscribed 'Hong Kong, 1841, April'

The hill shown in this watercolour is where the Government House, St John's Cathedral and the Government Offices are located today. This watercolour was done in April, 1841, three months after the British occupation when Hong Kong was still a barren island.

港島「政府山」景色，一八四一年
柯林斯畫
紙本水彩畫　23.6×32厘米
附有畫家署名及題識

此圖所繪畫之地方，乃今督憲府、聖約翰教堂及政府合署所在之山岡。是圖繪畫於一八四一年四月，開埠後僅三月，故岸上一片荒蕪。

4
Early View of Morrison Hill and Happy Valley from the Harbour, 1841
by John H. Collins
watercolour on paper, 22.5 × 32cm
signed and inscribed 'Valley at Hong Kong, May, 1841'

Morrison Hill, which has been levelled years ago, is shown in the foreground. Behind the hill is Happy Valley.

從港海眺望跑馬地及摩利臣山景色，一八四一年
柯林斯畫
紙本水彩畫　22.5×32厘米
附有畫家署名及題識

畫中前方山岡為摩利臣山，其背後為跑馬地，摩利臣山現已夷為平地。

5
European Officers Greeting Chinese Mandarins, circa 1843
artist unknown
watercolour on paper, 29 × 39.5cm

The Chinese Commissioner Keying arrived at Hong Kong to exchange the documents concerning the Treaty of Nanking with the British officials on June 26, 1843. This painting most probably recorded the scene when the mandarin was greeted by Sir Henry Pottinger at the Government House.

中英官員會面圖,約一八四三年
畫家佚名
紙本水彩畫 29×39.5厘米

此畫所見極可能是一八四三年六月廿六日欽差大臣耆英到港主持南京條約換文時,砵典乍爵士迎於督轅之情景。

6
Victoria from the Sea, circa 1846
by Lieutenant Walford T. Bellairs, R.N., circa 1794-1850
pencil and brown ink sketch on paper, 13 × 23cm
inscribed 'Hong Kong, Victoria Peak 1600'

Lieutenant Bellairs was a rather gifted amateur artist. During 1845 and 1846, he became the admiralty agent of the ship Lady Mary Wood, owned by the Peninsula and Oriental Steam Navigation Company. He visited Hong Kong in 1846 on board of this vessel.

從港海眺望港島，約一八四六年
貝萊爾斯畫(約一七九四至一八五〇)
紙本鉛筆及棕色墨素描　13×23厘米
附有畫家題識

貝萊爾斯少校是一位頗具天份的業餘畫家，一八四五至四六年間成爲鐵行輪船公司的瑪麗‧伍德夫人號的駐船專員，一八四六年到過香港。

7
Spring Gardens, 1846
by Murdoch Bruce
oil painting, 27.5 × 36cm

Murdoch Bruce, a talented watercolourist was the Inspector of Buildings and Overseer of Roads in the early years of Hong Kong. He has done a set of twelve paintings of Hong Kong which were later engraved into lithographs. This is by far the only oil by Bruce found.

春園風光，一八四六年
布魯士畫
油畫　27.5×36厘米

布魯士在香港開埠初年曾先後任建築物督察及道路監督之職，他是優秀的水彩畫家，曾繪畫了一套十二幅香港風光畫，刻印為版畫。這是布氏僅見的油畫。

8
The Waterfront, Central District from the Harbour, 1846
by George Chinnery, 1774-1852
oil painting, 35.6 × 57.1cm

George Chinnery had resided in Macau for 27 years. It is known that he visited Hong Kong only once in 1846. As a result, he executed only a few paintings on the scenery of Hong Kong. Oil painting of this kind is very rare.

從港海眺望中區海旁，一八四六年
錢納利畫（一七七四至一八五二）
油畫　35.6×57.1厘米

錢納利在澳門居留了二十七年，祇在一八四六年來過香港，住了半年，所以錢氏繪畫的香港風景畫數量不多，而油畫更彌足珍貴。

9
The Waterfront, Central District from the Harbour, 1846
by George Chinnery, 1774-1852
pencil and ink sketch on paper, 21.6 × 43.2cm

Dent & Co. and Lindsay's Company are seen along the waterfront. The hill beyond where a flag is seen flying is Pedder's Hill, the site where the Harbour Master's Office was located. Pedder's Hill was named after Lieutenant William Pedder, the first Harbour Master of Hong Kong.

從港海眺望中區海旁，一八四六年
錢納利畫(一七七四至一八五二)
紙本鉛筆及鋼筆素描　21.6×43.2厘米

畫中可看到寶順及林賽洋行，其上山岡豎一旗杆乃畢打山港務局所在。畢打山乃以本港首位港務局長畢打命名。

10
View of Queen's Road Central, 1846
attributed to George Chinnery, 1774-1852
pencil and brown ink sketch on paper, 20.4 × 31cm

Queen's Road is one of the roads which were constructed right after the British occupation. The first building shown in the left is most probably the old Hong Kong Club building (site of the present King's Theatre). In front of it is the Post Office (site of the present China Building).

皇后大道中街景,一八四六年
傳爲錢納利所畫(一七七四至一八五二)
紙本鉛筆及棕色墨素描 20.4×31厘米

皇后大道是本港開埠後最早興築的街道之一。畫中左方第一幢建築極可能是舊香港會所(即今娛樂戲院所在),其對面爲郵政局(今華人行)。

11
View of the Harbour Master's Office on Pedder's Hill, 1846
attributed to George Chinnery, 1774-1852
pencil and brown ink sketch on paper, 21.8 × 31cm

Wyndham Street, just completed is seen in the foreground. The vicinity shown in the picture was later developed into a commercial and residential area.

畢打山港務局，一八四六年
傳爲錢納利所畫(一七七四至一八五二)
紙本鉛筆及棕色墨素描　21.8×31厘米

圖中前方剛開鑿之馬路爲雲咸街，畢打山後闢爲商業及住宅區。

12
View of the Waterfront, Central District, from the East, 1846
attributed to George Chinnery, 1774-1852
pencil and brown ink sketch on paper, 19.7 × 29.7cm

This view most probably shows the juncture at Queensway and Queen's Road Central.

西眺中區海旁景色，一八四六年
傳為錢納利所畫（一七七四至一八五二）
紙本鉛筆及棕色墨素描　19.7×29.7厘米

圖中所見可能是中區海旁近金鐘道與大道中交界處。

13
The Hong Kong Club, circa 1846
by George Strachan, lithographed by Millar
coloured lithograph, 26.5 × 42.5cm

The painting shows the old Hong Kong Club building, founded in 1846. Hong Kong Club was later moved to the new site in Connaught Road in 1898. George Strachan was in fact the architect of this old building.

香港會所，約一八四六年
斯特羅恩畫，米勒刻印
設色石版畫　26.5×42.5厘米

圖中所見之建築物，乃舊香港會所，該會所成立於一八四六年，至一八九八年遷至干諾道新址。本畫畫家斯特羅恩，乃舊香港會所之建築師。

14
View of Spring Gardens, 1850s
by Dr Thomas B. Watson, 1815-1860
pencil and brown ink sketch on paper, 22.5 × 31.5 cm

The Spring Gardens was a high class residential area in the 1840s to 1850s. It was located in the vicinity of the present Queen's Road East and the Hopewell Centre area.

春園一角，一八五〇年代
屈臣醫生畫（一八一五至一八六〇）
紙本鉛筆及棕色墨素描　22.5×31.5厘米

春園即今之灣仔皇后大道東近合和中心附近地區，十九世紀四十至五十年代爲環境優美之高尚住宅區。

15
The Waterfront, Central District, Hong Kong, 1850s
by Dr Thomas B. Watson, 1815-1860
pencil and watercolour on paper, 19 × 23cm
inscribed 'Hong Kong'

Dr Watson was one of the followers of George Chinnery. He moved from Scotland to Macau in 1845, where he met Chinnery and became his friend and physician and later attended him on his deathbed. He returned to Scotland in 1858, and died two years later.

港島中區海旁景色，一八五〇年代
屈臣醫生畫（一八一五至一八六〇）
紙本鉛筆水彩畫　19×23厘米
附有畫家題識

屈臣醫生是錢納利的高足之一，他在一八四五年從英國移居澳門，結識錢納利，並成爲他的朋友。錢氏臨終時，屈臣隨侍在側，在料理完其師之身後事，移居香港。一八五八年回國，兩年後於蘇格蘭去世。

16
View of the Central District, Hong Kong, from the East, circa 1850s
by Lieutenant Chambeyron
coloured engraving, 14.5 × 32cm

This is a painting of the Central District of Hong Kong by the French lieutenant Chambeyron. It was used as an illustration in the French edition of *Universal Journal*. It can be seen from the painting that reclamation works had not started yet.

西眺港島中區景色，約一八五〇年代
張伯羅恩中校畫
設色金屬刻版畫　14.5×32厘米

這是法國張伯羅恩中校繪畫的香港中區風景畫。是法文版環球畫報的插圖。從是畫所見，沿岸尚未進行填海工程。

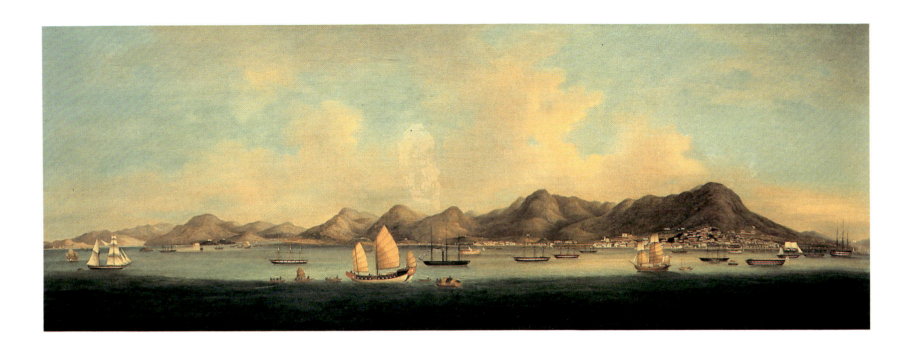

17
Victoria from the North, 1855-60
artist unknown
oil painting, 53.2 × 147.5cm

This view extends from Lei Yu Mun to the western end of Hong Kong Island. Some of the well-known landmarks which appear are Jardines premises at East Point; Morrison Institute; St John's Cathedral; Government Offices and Government House.

從北方眺望維多利亞城，一八五五至六〇年
畫家佚名
油畫　53.2×147.5厘米

此畫展示從鯉魚門至港島西區的景色、可辨認的建築有東角的渣甸洋行、馬禮遜教育會、聖約翰教堂、輔政司署及督憲府。

18
Victoria and the Peak, 1855-60
artist unknown
gouache on paper, 44.1 × 77.1cm

The painting clearly shows the St John's Cathedral, Government House, Bishop's House, Roman Cathedral and a pair of dome-shaped roof-top. Dent & Co. can be seen near the coast.

維多利亞城及山頂，一八五五至六〇年
畫家佚名
紙本水粉畫　44.1×77.1厘米

畫中可清楚看到聖約翰教堂、督憲府、會督府、羅馬天主堂及其一對圓拱形之屋頂，海旁還可看到寶順洋行。

19
The Waterfront, Central District, Hong Kong, late 1850s
by Marciano A. Baptista
watercolour on paper, 33 × 59cm

This is a masterpiece by Baptista whose watercolour distinguishes itself in its accuracy of depiction. The numerous buildings along the shore between Russell's Company and the Peninsula and Oriental Steam Navigation Company can be clearly seen.

港島中區海旁景色，一八五〇年代晚期
巴普蒂斯塔畫
紙本水彩畫　33×59厘米

這是巴普蒂斯塔的傑作。巴氏的水彩畫以精確見稱，此畫可清楚看到海旁從旗昌洋行至鐵行輪船公司的大小建築物。

20
View of Queen's Road and Victoria Harbour from Pedder's Hill, late 1850s
by Marciano A. Baptista
watercolour on paper, 50 × 69.2cm

Queen's Road Central is shown in the foreground. The two most magnificent buildings in Central at that time, Lindsay's Company (right) and Dent & Co. (left), are depicted in the painting together with Pedder Street in the left leading to the coast.

從畢打山俯瞰皇后大道及港海景色，一八五〇年代晚期
巴普蒂斯塔畫
紙本水彩畫 50×69.2厘米

畫中前方是皇后大道中。畫面可看到當時中區最宏偉的兩所建築物：林賽洋行（右方）及寶順洋行（左方）。畫的左方還可以看到通往海邊的畢打街。

21
View of Hong Kong Island from Tsim Sha Tsui, late 1850s
attributed to Marciano A. Baptista
oil painting, 45.7 × 59.7cm

In the foreground is Tsim Sha Tsui. Hong Kong Island and the Harbour are shown in the background.

從尖沙咀眺望港島，一八五〇年代晚期
傳爲巴普蒂斯塔所畫
油畫　45.7×59.7厘米

畫之前方爲尖沙咀，後方是港島及港海。

22
A House in the Mid-levels, Hong Kong, early 1860s
attributed to Marciano A. Baptista
watercolour on paper, 30.5 × 43cm

The road in the foreground is most probably Caine Road. The flag of the Government House can be seen in the left. A sedan chair seen in the picture was once the usual means by which people travelled around in the Mid-levels before the Peak Tram began operation.

港島半山一洋房，一八六〇年代初期
傳為巴普蒂斯塔所畫
紙本水彩畫　30.5×43厘米

畫中前方之道路，似為堅道，左方可看到督憲府之旗杆。屋子前方還可看到一乘山兜，在纜車尚未啟行前，半山一帶來往多仰賴山兜。

23
View of the Central and Victoria Harbour from the Mid-levels, early 1860.
by Marciano A. Baptista
watercolour on paper, 40.5 × 57cm

The road in the foreground is most probably Caine Road. The vicinity of Wellington Street and Cochrane street is seen in the middle ground with the dome structure of the first Roman Catholic Cathedral clearly depicted.

從半山俯瞰中區及港海景色，一八六〇年代初期
巴普蒂斯塔畫
紙本水彩畫　40.5×57厘米

畫中前方所見之道路，極可能是堅道，其下為中區威靈頓街及閣麟街一帶，可清楚看到香港第一間羅馬天主堂之圓拱形屋頂。

24
Hong Kong Island From Tsim Sha Tsui, early 1860s
by R. Shannon
watercolour on paper, 14 × 22.3cm

The foreground area covered with numerous military camps is Tsim Sha Tsui. Hong Kong Island is in the background. The signal station on the Peak was erected in 1861.

從尖沙咀眺望港島景色，一八六〇年代初期
香農畫
紙本水彩畫　14×22.3厘米

畫之前方是尖沙咀，滿佈軍營，後面是香港島，山頂上的訊號台，建於一八六一年。

25
View of Hong Kong Island from Kowloon Peninsula, early 1860s
artist unknown
oil painting, 30.6 × 71.8cm

The foreground of the painting shows the area around Tsim Sha Tsui and Yau Ma Tei. The bay in the left is the present Chatham Road.

從九龍半島眺望港島，一八六〇年代初期
畫家佚名
油畫　30.6×71.8厘米

畫中前方可看到尖沙咀及油麻地一帶地區，畫之左方之海灣約相等於現在之漆咸道。

26
View of the Racecourse and Morrison Hill from the Mid-levels, 1863
by Robert G.D. Tosswill
pencil and watercolour on paper, 17.5 × 25.2cm
inscribed 'The Racecourse from the Haunted House, Hong Kong, March 15 1863. R.G.D.T. 99 Regt'

Happy Valley is seen in the foreground with the Morrison Memorial School to the left and the Bowrington town down below. As a military topographer, Tosswill has rendered the topography with great accuracy.

從半山俯瞰馬場及摩利臣山，一八六三年
托斯威爾畫
紙本鉛筆及水彩畫　17.5×25.2厘米
附有畫家題識

此畫前方為跑馬地，左方山岡上為馬禮遜紀念學校，山下為寶靈頓城，即今之鵝頸。本畫畫家托斯威爾是一位隨軍繪圖員，故繪畫地形，異常準確。

27
The Flagstaff House, Hong Kong, 1860s
artist unknown
watercolour on paper, 17.5 × 25cm

Built in 1844 and completed in 1846, the Flagstaff House has been the residence of the Military Commander of Hong Kong. It is being converted into a museum for the display of teaware. The Government House and St John's Cathedral could also be seen to the left of the picture.

香港旗杆屋，一八六〇年代
畫家佚名
紙本水彩畫　17.5×25厘米

旗杆屋興築於一八四四年，竣工於一八四六年，一直是駐港英軍司令的官邸。該具有歷史價值之建築物將改裝為茶具文物館。畫的左方還可看到督憲府及聖約翰教堂。

28
The Rev. Raimondi Taking a Rest on the Way to Stanley, circa 1860s
by Edward Hildebrandt
coloured engraving, 16 × 24cm

The Rev. Raimondi became Bishop of Hong Kong in 1874. During his 36 years of stay in Hong Kong, he went to remote parts of Hong Kong to preach to the village people. Raimondi died in Hong Kong in 1894.

高主教赴赤柱途中小憩,約一八六〇年代
希爾德布蘭德畫
設色金屬刻版畫　16×24厘米

高主教於一八七四年晉升為香港教區主教,一八九四年在港逝世,前後在香港居住了三十六年。早年常不辭勞苦到本港較荒僻地區傳教。

29
Queen's Road, Hong Kong, 1860s
by Edward Hildebrandt
reproduction of a watercolour, 27.5 × 38.2 cm
signed and inscribed 'Hong Kong'

The painting probably shows Queen's Road West, where early Chinese residents in Hong Kong congregated. The buildings are different in style from those seen in the European residential area in Hong Kong.

皇后大道,一八六〇年代
希爾德布蘭德畫
水彩畫複本 27.5×38.2厘米
附有畫家署名及題識

相信是皇后大道西,圖中所見爲華人聚居地區,其建築與西人住宅區迥異。

30
Social Activities in Hong Kong, 1870s
by H.N. Shore
pen and ink sketch on paper, 19 × 15cm
inscribed 'Hong Kong Society'

This is a portrayal of the life of the westerners in Hong Kong. This is one of the paintings by Shore which shows a scene of the daily life of the westerners in Hong Kong.

香港的社交活動，一八七〇年代
蕭爾畫
紙本鉛筆及鋼筆素描　19×15厘米
附有畫家題識

這是香港西人生活的寫照。蕭爾繪畫了一些描繪洋人在香港生活情況的素描，這是其中的一幅。

31
Extensive View of Macau from the Sea, 1793
by William Alexander, 1767-1816
watercolour on paper, 25.2 × 40.2 cm

William Alexander was a famous British watercolourist. He served as an a draughtsman in Lord Macartney's embassy to China. This is a rate watercolour which he executed when the embassy reached Macau.

從外海眺望澳門景色，一七九三年
亞歷山大畫(一七六七至一八一六)
紙本水彩畫 25.2×40.2厘米

威廉・亞歷山大是英國著名的水彩畫家，他曾隨馬戛爾尼使節團訪華，作隨團畫師。這是他經澳門時所繪畫的水彩原作，極為珍貴。

32
View of the Central Part of Macau from Penha Hill, late 18th century
artist unknown
oil painting, 35.5 × 54.3cm

The development of Macau in the eighteenth and the nineteenth centuries can be revealed by comparing this painting with No. 60.

從西望洋山俯瞰澳門中部,十八世紀晚期
畫家佚名
油畫 35.5×54.3厘米

與圖六十比較,可看到澳門在十八及十九世紀的發展。

33
View of the Praya Grande from the South, Macau, 1824
by Captain Robert Elliot R.N.
pencil drawing on paper, 40.5 × 88.5cm
inscribed 'Macao October 1824 by Capt Elliot, R.N.'

Captain Robert Elliot is an amateur marine painter of considerable talent who exhibited paintings at the Royal Academy in 1784 to 1791. He visited India and China during the period between 1822 to 1824.

北眺澳門南灣景色，一八二四年
埃利奧特上校畫
紙本鉛筆素描　40.5×88.5厘米
附有畫家題識

埃利奧特上校是一位頗有藝術天份的業餘畫家，一八二二至二四年間隨軍到過印度及中國，他的傑作曾於一七八四至九一年間在皇家畫院展出。

34
View of the Praya Grande from the South, Macau, 1824
by Captain Robert Elliot R.N.
pencil drawing on paper, 40.5 × 88.5cm
inscribed 'Macao October 1824. Drawn by Capt Elliot R.N., my father's house with balcony'

These two exquisite pencil sketches from the Chater Collection distinguish themselves by their high degree of accuracy. In the foreground where a flag post is found is the Chinese customs office. Both the office and the post were removed in 1849.

南眺澳門南灣景色，一八二四年
埃利奧特上校畫
紙本鉛筆素描　40.5×88.5厘米
附有畫家題識

這兩幅鉛筆素描，繪畫精確，是遮打藏畫現存的精品之一。畫中前方所見旗杆高聳處乃中國海關設立之稅館，該稅館及旗杆在一八四九年撤去。

35
The Misericordia and Senate Square, Macau, 1832
by George Chinnery, 1774-1852
pencil drawing on paper, 11.7 × 17.8cm
inscribed 'The Misericordia & Senate Square, Macao, 28.1.1832'

The Santa Casa da Misericordia is the oldest charitable organization in Macau. This building was constructed during the late eighteenth century and the facade was added in the next century. Fort Monte is seen in the background.

澳門仁慈堂及議事廳前廣場，一八三二年
錢納利畫（一七七四至一八五二）
紙本鉛筆素描　11.7×17.8厘米
附有畫家題識

仁慈堂是澳門歷史最悠久的慈善團體。目前的建築興建於十八世紀晚期，建築物的前壁則十九世紀才興建。後方是大砲台。

36
View of the Church of St Paul from the Waterfront, circa early 1830s
attributed to Marciano A. Baptista
watercolour on paper, 20.5 × 26 cm

從海邊眺望聖保祿教堂(大三巴),約一八三〇年代初期
傳為巴普蒂斯塔所作
紙本水彩畫 20.5×26厘米

Many drawings have been made from time to time to depict the facade, but there are very few paintings which show the original appearance of the church before the fire. This watercolour showing the original structure with its facade and church tower is a rare and valuable pictorial record of the church before the fire of 1835.

現存繪畫聖保祿教堂前壁的畫不少,但清楚展示未焚前之教堂原貌的繪畫則極為罕見。是畫描繪了一八三五年大火前聖保祿教堂的建築,前壁及鐘樓清晰可見,是極罕貴的圖畫紀錄。

37
Fisherman's Squatters and a Chinese Temple, 1838
by Auguste Borget, 1809-1877
oil painting, 32.8 × 51cm

August Borget lived in Macau for half a year in 1838 and 1839 when he met George Chinnery. Traces of Chinnery's influence can be found in this painting in the form, line quality and the figures.

艇戶及廟宇，一八三八年
波塞爾畫(一八〇九至一八七七)
油畫　32.8×51厘米

波塞爾在一八三八至三九年間，在澳門居住了半年，曾向英國畫家錢納利請教繪畫技法。是畫所見，其所畫之人物，線條及造型均有錢納利的影子。

38
Fisherman's Squatters, Macau, 1838
by Auguste Borget, 1809-1877
pencil drawing on paper, 22 × 36cm
signed and inscribed in French, Boatman's Dwellings in Macau

This painting has been lithographed by E. Ciceri.

澳門的漁民棚屋,一八三八年
波塞爾畫(一八〇九至一八七七)
紙本鉛筆素描 22×36厘米
附有畫家署名及題識

是畫曾由西塞里刻印爲石版畫。

39
The Square Outside the Ma Kok Temple, 1838
by Auguste Borget, 1809-1877, lithographed by E. Ciceri
coloured lithograph, 29 × 41.5cm

Situated at the base of Barra Hill, the temple was erected by fisherfolks dedicated to the goddess Tin Hau (Heavenly Queen) during the reign of Wanli (1573-1621) in the Ming Dynasty.

媽閣廟外的廣場，一八三八年
波塞爾畫（一八〇九至一八七七），西塞里刻印
設色石版畫　29×41.5厘米

媽閣廟位於澳門巴勒山山腳，是漁民為奉祀天后而在明朝萬曆年間（一五七三至一六二一）興築的。

40
The Church of St Domingo, Macau, 1838
by Auguste Borget, 1809-1877, lithographed by E. Ciceri
coloured lithograph, 19 × 13.1cm

The church which is situated at close proximity to the Santa Casa da Misericordia was built in the early seventeenth century by Spanish fraírs. The square in front of the church has long been the busiest spot in the city.

澳門板樟堂外貌，一八三八年
波塞爾畫(一八〇九至一八七七)，西塞里刻印
設色石版畫　19×13.1厘米

板樟堂在仁慈堂附近，是西班牙教士在十七世紀初興建的。長久以來，教堂前的廣場是澳門最繁盛的地方。

41
The Ma Kok Temple, Macau, circa 1838
by William Prinsep
oil painting, 50.8 × 76.2cm

William Prinsep was an amateur artist who studied with George Chinnery. Although the family of Prinsep used to be government officials in India, Prinsep himself became a merchant. Many excellent watercolours were done during his visit to Macau and Hong Kong along the South China coast.

澳門媽閣廟,約一八三八年
普林塞普畫
油畫 50.8×76.2厘米

普林塞普是一位業餘畫家,曾隨錢納利習畫。普氏家族世代於印度做官,普林塞普則是一位商人,曾到過華南沿岸的澳門及廣州,並繪畫了不少出色的水彩畫。

42
Fisherman at Work on the Praya Grande, 1825-1852
by George Chinnery, 1774-1852
oil painting, 26.7 × 45.7cm

The fisherfolk was one of Chinnery's most favourite subjects. This painting shows the fishermen at work at the Praya Grande.

濠江漁歌，一八二五至五二年間
錢納利畫（一七七四至一八五二）
油畫　26.7×45.7厘米

漁民是錢納利最喜愛的題材，是畫繪畫了漁民在南灣作業的情景。

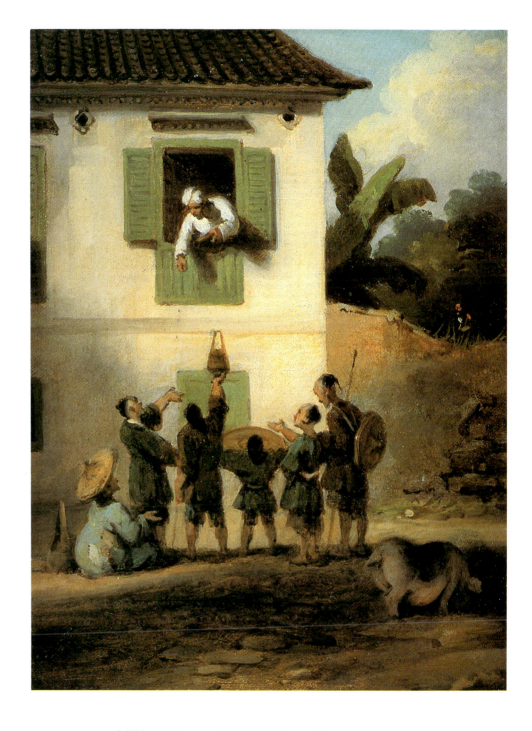

43
Street Traders, Macau, 1825-1852
by George Chinnery, 1774-1852
oil painting, 22.9 × 17.8cm

George Chinnery had a keen interest in observing the daily life of the Chinese people around him. The hawkers, beggars, fishermen and blacksmiths are all vividly depicted under his confident brush.

澳門的小販，一八二五至五二年間
錢納利畫(一七七四至一八五二)
油畫　22.9×17.8厘米

錢納利對華人的生活動態非常留意，畫筆下的小販、乞丐、漁民、鐵匠等小人物無不栩栩如生。

44
Fishermen Beside a Boat, 1825-1852
by George Chinnery, 1774-1852
oil painting 16.4 × 21.5cm

Under Chinnery's brush, the fisherfolks, whether they are men, women or children, are animated with great interest.

艇旁漁民，一八二五至五二年間
錢納利畫（一七七四至一八五二）
油畫　16.4×21.5厘米

錢納利筆下的漁民，無論是男子、婦女與小孩都栩栩欲活，極富生趣。

45
A Fishing Junk in an Inlet, Macau, 1825-1852
by George Chinnery, 1774-1852
pen and brown ink and watercolour on paper, 15 × 24cm

This painting shows the idyllic mood of the Inner Harbour. The shimmering ripples reflecting the silhouettes of the sailboat culminate in a sense of harmony and beauty. The flag-post of the Ma Kok Temple can be seen in the foreground.

濠江帆影,一八二五至五二年間
錢納利畫(一七七四至一八五二)
紙本棕色墨及水彩畫　15×24厘米

是畫繪畫了澳門內港的旖旎風光,波光帆影,具有柔和的美感。前方還可看到媽閣廟的幡杆。

46
The Franciscan Convent at Macau, 1825-1852
by George Chinnery, 1774-1852
pencil and brown ink sketch on paper, 21 × 30.4cm

The St Franciscan Convent was demolished in 1864 and was replaced by military barracks. Next to it is the Fortress of St Francisco.

澳門聖芳濟修院，一八二五至五二年間
錢納利畫(一七七四至一八五二)
紙本鉛筆及棕色墨素描　21×30.4厘米

聖芳濟修院在一八六四年拆卸，改為兵房。其旁為嘉思欄砲台。

47
The Ruins of St Paul's Church, Macau, 1837-1852
by George Chinnery, 1774-1852
pencil and brown ink sketch on paper, 16.5 × 21cm

The painting shows the site of the Church of St Paul in Macau. Situated at the foot of Monte Fort, the church was built in 1602 by the Portuguese and Japanese Christian followers and its scale was unsurpassed in the Far East. However, in 1835, both the church and its college caught fire and were burnt to the ground. Only the facade was left for people to ponder upon its past.

澳門聖保祿教堂遺跡，一八三七至五二年間
錢納利畫（一七七四至一八五二）
紙本鉛筆及棕色墨素描　16.5×21厘米

圖中所見乃澳門聖保祿教堂（大三巴）遺跡。該教堂位於中央砲台之山麓，是在一六○二年由葡人及日本人合力興建的。規模之大，冠絕東亞。一八三五年，教堂及所附之書院失火，整幢建築化成灰燼，祇剩下前面門樓，供人憑弔。

48
View of the Praya Grande from the North, 1840s
by George Chinnery, 1774-1852
oil painting, 45.7 × 87.6cm

This painting shows the scenery looking south from the northern end of the Praya Grande. Penha Hill is seen at the far end. Figures and animals are scattered in the landscape which was animated with human activities.

從北方眺望澳門南灣景色，一八四〇年代
錢納利畫（一七七四至一八五二）
油畫 45.7×87.6厘米

此畫繪畫的是從南灣的北端向南眺望的景色，南灣盡頭處是主教山，畫中穿插了不同的人物，還有各類禽畜，極富生活氣息。

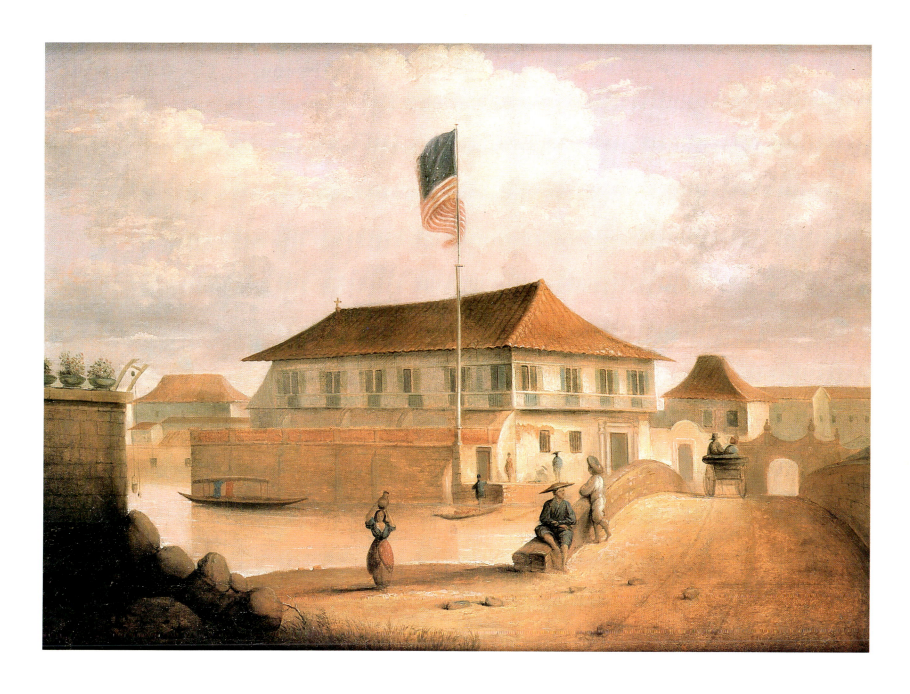

49
American Mission in Macau, 1844-1852
by George Chinnery, 1774-1852
oil painting, 45.7 × 61cm

The American diplomat Caleb Cushing reached Macau in February 1844 appointed as diplomatic envoy, he signed the Treaty of Wangxia with Keying in July. Cushing's house in Macau became the first American legation in China.

澳門的美國使館,一八四四至五二年間
錢納利畫(一七七四至一八五二)
油畫 45.7×61厘米

美國外交家顧聖在一八四四年二月抵澳,同年七月,以專使身份與耆英簽訂中美望廈條約。顧氏在澳門的居所乃美國在中國的第一間使館。

50
The Franciscan Convent and Guia Fort, 1840s
by James, T. Caldwell
pencil and watercolour on paper, 20 × 31.5cm

Caldwell was a commodore of the Royal Navy, as well as an amateur painter. He came to the Far East in his official capacity in 1842 and died in the navy in 1849.

澳門聖芳濟修院及松山砲台，一八四〇年代
考德維爾畫
紙本鉛筆及水彩畫 20×31.5厘米

畫家考德維爾是一位業餘畫家，他是英國皇家海軍的准將，一八四二年隨軍至遠東，一八四九年在軍中去世。

51
The Southern End of the Praya Grande, Macau, 1848
by William Prinsep
watercolour on paper, 25.8 × 36cm
inscribed 'July 48'

The hill shown in the right is Penha Hill with a church erected upon it. A city will extends down the hill reaching the coast where the Fort of Bomparto is located.

澳門南灣南端，一八四八年
普林塞普畫
紙本水彩畫　25.8×36厘米
附有畫家題識

畫中右方山頂為西望洋山，上築教堂，城牆蜿蜒而下，海邊為西砲台。

52
View of Penha Hill, Macau, late 1840s to early 1850s
by Dr Thomas B. Watson
pencil and brown ink and watercolour on paper, 21.7 × 31cm

Penha Hill is sixty-nine metres high, the third highest in Macau. A fort was once built on the hill. The fort was later replaced by Our Lady of Penha Church in 1622 which was rebuilt to become the residence of the Bishop in 1935.

西望洋山風光，一八四〇年代晚期至一八五〇年代初期
屈臣醫生畫（一八一五至一八六〇）
紙本鉛筆及棕色墨水彩畫　21.7×31厘米

西望洋山高六十九米，乃澳門第三高岡。最初曾興築砲台，一六二二年該址建了一座西望洋聖母堂，一九三五年改建爲主敎府，故此山又名主敎山。

53
The Fortress of St Francisco, Macau, late 1840s to early 1850s
by Dr Thomas B. Watson, 1815-1860
pencil, ink and watercolour on paper, 21 × 29.5cm
inscribed 'Macau'

Directly facing the Sap Chi Mun (Cross Gate), this part of the Fort of St Francisco occupied a strategic position. Above the fort is the Fransciscan Convent.

澳門嘉思欄砲台，一八四〇年代晚期至一八五〇年代初期
屈臣醫生畫(一八一五至一八六〇)
紙本鉛筆及鋼筆水彩畫　21×29.5厘米
附有畫家題識

此為嘉思欄砲台的一角，面臨十字門，形勢險要，砲台上方為聖芳濟教堂。

54
The Northern Part of the Praya Grande from the South, late 1840s to early 1850s
by Dr Thomas B. Watson, 1815-1860
pencil drawing on paper, 21.8 × 32cm

The building to the left of the picture is Monte Fort. Down below the hill is the Cathedral. Guia Hill is shown in the right. At the far end of the Praya Grande are the Fortress of St Francisco and Franciscan Convent.

北眺南灣北角景色，一八四〇年代晚期至一八五〇年代初期
屈臣醫生畫（一八一五至一八六〇）
紙本鉛筆素描　21.8×32厘米

畫之左方是大砲台，高阜下方是大堂，右方之山岡是東望洋山，也稱松山，南灣盡處是嘉思欄砲台及聖芳濟修道院。

55
Extensive View of Macau from Penha Hill, 1852
by Dr Thomas B. Watson, 1815-1860
pencil and brown ink and watercolour on paper, 21 × 31.5cm
inscribed '15 Dec., 52'

This is a view of the Praya Grande looking north from Penha Hill. On the right is Guia Hill and near the centre is Monte Fort. The fluidity of line and the harmony of the palette distinguishes itself as one of the finest works by Dr Watson.

從西望洋山俯瞰澳門景色，一八五二年
屈臣醫生畫(一八一五至一八六〇)
紙本鉛筆棕色墨水彩畫　21×31.5厘米
附有繪畫年份

畫中所見是從主教山麓北眺南灣的景色，最右方是松山，近中央位置是大砲台，此畫線條流暢，色調柔和，是屈臣醫生的精彩作品。

56
View of the Northern Part of the Praya Grande from St Peter's Fort, Macau, early 1850s
by Thomas B. Watson, 1815-1860
watercolour on paper 18.6 × 27.5cm

Looking north from St Peter's Fort, this is a view showing the northern part of the Praya Grande. Guia Hill is in the background.

澳門南灣聖彼德小砲台，一八五〇年代初期
屈臣醫生畫（一八一五至一八六〇）
紙本水彩畫　18.6×27.5厘米

圖中所見乃從聖彼德小砲台北眺南環北角之景色，後方是松山（東望洋山）。

57
The Praya Grande from the North, 1856
by Marciano A. Baptista
watercolour on paper, 37 × 65cm
signed and inscribed '1856'

M. Baptista was a Macau born Portuguese. He studied with George Chinnery in his early years. In the 1850s, he moved to Hong Kong and served as an art teacher in a secondary school. Baptista's watercolour shows great stylistic kindrance to that of his teacher. The crowd below the tree in front of the painting shows strong hints of Chinnery's influence especially in the treatment of the figural form. Signed paintings by Baptista like this one are rare.

南眺澳門南灣景色，一八五六年
巴普蒂斯塔畫
紙本水彩畫　37×65厘米
附有畫家署名及繪畫年份

巴普蒂斯塔是澳門出生的葡萄牙人。早年隨錢納利習畫，五〇年代移居香港，在中學當美術教師。巴氏的水彩畫，模倣乃師作風，畫中前方樹下的人群，造型處理明顯帶有錢納利的風格。巴氏署名之作不多見，這畫附有其親筆署名，相當難得。

58
The Ma Kok Temple, Macau, 1860
by R.V. Decker, lithographed by W. Korn & Co.
chromolithograph, 31.5 × 46.5cm

This painting shows one of the most popular architecture in Macau — the frontal view of the Ma Kok Temple. This elegantly coloured lithograph is both delightful and attractive.

澳門媽閣廟全景，一八六〇年
德克爾畫，科恩公司刻印
設色石版畫　31.5×46.5厘米

是畫清楚地展示了澳門最膾炙人口的古建築之一——媽閣廟的正面景貌。此版畫設色雅麗，清新可喜。

59
The Praya Grande from the South at Sunset, 1862
by Edward Hildebrandt
watercolour on paper, 25 × 38cm
inscribed 'Macao, 1862'

The Fort of St Peter stands at the left of the lowest plane of the picture. Behind the fort is the Cathedral which was built between 1844 to 1850. To the right is the St Franciscan Convent which was later demolished. The Fortress of St Francisco is at its side.

南灣夕照，一八六二年
希爾德布蘭德畫
紙本水彩畫　25×38厘米
附有畫家題識

畫中左前方是聖彼德小砲台，其後方是一八四四至五〇年間興築的大堂，最右方還可看到拆卸前夕的聖芳濟修院，其旁爲嘉思欄砲台。

60
Panoramic View of Macau from Penha Hill, circa 1870
artist unknown
gouache on paper, 49.5 × 113.5cm

This gouache painting stands out among the China trade paintings in its accurate depiction of the landscape. It shows a panoramic view of Macau looking north of Penha Hill. Important landmarks like the Church of St Paul, Monte Fort, the Cathedral and the Church of St Lawrence can all be identified.

從主教山俯瞰澳門全景，約一八七〇年
畫家佚名
紙本水粉畫　49.5×113.5厘米

這是一幅繪畫得特別精確的水粉畫，當是中國外銷畫家的傑作。畫中所見是從主教山向北俯瞰的景色，澳門全市盡入眼底。大三巴、大砲台、大堂、風順堂等濠江著名建築均可一一辨認。